CIPS STUDY MATTERS

DIPLOMA IN PURCHASING AND SUPPLY

REVISION NOTES

Negotiating and contracting in procurement and supply

© Profex Publishing Limited, 2012

Printed and distributed by:
The Chartered Institute of Purchasing & Supply, Easton House, Easton on the Hill, Stamford,
Lincolnshire PE9 3NZ
Tel: +44 (0) 1780 756 777
Fax: +44 (0) 1780 751 610
Email: info@cips.org
Website: www.cips.org

First edition October 2012

Contents

Preface

Welcome to your Revision Notes.

Your Revision Notes are a summarised version of the material contained in your Course Book. If you find that the Revision Notes refer to material that you do not recollect clearly, you should refer back to the Course Book to refresh your memory.

There is space at the end of each chapter in your Revision Notes where you can enter your own notes for reference.

A note on style

Throughout your Study Packs you will find that we use the masculine form of personal pronouns. This convention is adopted purely for the sake of stylistic convenience – we just don't like saying 'he/she' all the time. Please don't think this reflects any kind of bias or prejudice.

October 2012

CHAPTER 1

Developing Commercial Agreements

Commercial agreements

The law of contract is concerned with four basic questions.

- Is there a contract in existence?
- Is the agreement one which the law should recognise and enforce?
- When do the obligations of the parties come to an end?
- What remedies are available for an injured party?

A key requirement is the clear statement and accurate alignment of:

- Exactly **what the buyer wants**
- What the supplier is offering, or agrees to supply.

The buying organisation will seek to establish a detailed description of its requirements which can be communicated to potential suppliers.

- Specifications (of various types)
- Service level agreements (added to the specification of services)
- Contract terms
- Key performance indicators

A requirement can be signalled to prospective, pre-qualified or approved suppliers in various ways, depending on the sourcing policies of the organisation for particular types of purchase. For routine, low-value purchases or re-buys, for example, there may be framework agreements or call-off contracts in place. Or the buyer may simply be able to refer to approved suppliers' catalogues or price lists and make one off purchases.

For more modified, new, non-standard or high-value requirements, the buyer may have to initiate negotiations with, or solicit proposals from, one or more suppliers, in order to develop an agreed understanding of what the buyer requires, and what the supplier is able to offer: in other words, the basis for a contract.

Quotation and tender documents

One approach to initiating dealings with a supplier is to send an enquiry, 'request for information', 'request for quotation' (RFQ) or 'request for proposal' (RFP) to one or more suppliers. Unsolicited proposals or quotations may also be sent in by suppliers.

A standard enquiry or RFQ form will typically set out the details of the requirement.

- The contact details of the purchaser
- A reference number to use in reply, and date by which to reply
- The quantity and description of goods or services required
- The required place and date of delivery
- The buyer's standard (and any special) terms and conditions of purchase
- Terms of payment

There are ethical issues in the use of requests for quotation, which may be the subject of procurement ethical codes.

The organisation may prefer to use a more formalised *competitive bidding* or tendering procedure, in which pre-qualified suppliers are issued with an invitation to tender (ITT).

Approaches to tendering:

- Open tendering
- Selective tendering
- Restricted open tenders

The general principle is that the successful tender will be the one with the lowest price or the 'most economically advantageous tender'.

Specifications

A specification can be simply defined as a statement of the requirements to be satisfied in the supply of a product or service.

Purpose of specification:

- Define the requirement
- Communicate the requirement clearly to suppliers
- Minimise risk and cost associated with doubt, ambiguity, misunderstanding or dispute

Two main types of specification: conformance specification and performance specification.

- With a **conformance specification** (eg drawing, blueprint, chemical formula), the buyer details exactly what the required product, part or material must *consist of*.
- A **performance (or functional) specification** is a relatively brief document in which the buyer describes what he expects a part or material to be able to *achieve*.

Advantages of performance specifications:

- Easier and cheaper to draft

- Does not depend on the technical knowledge of the buyer
- Suppliers can use their full expertise, technologies and innovative capacity
- A greater share of specification risk is borne by the supplier
- The potential supply base is wider than with a conformance specification

Services present buyers with additional problems.

- Services are intangible and lack 'inspectability'.
- Services are variable.
- Services are provided in 'real time'.
- Many services can only be performed in particular locations.
- A service may be procured for a long contract period.

Key performance indicators

Supplier performance measurement is the assessment and comparison of a supplier's current performance against:

- Defined performance criteria
- Previous performance
- The performance of other comparable organisations or standard benchmarks

Performance measurement is important because it supports the planning and control of operations and relationships. Performance measures, or key performance indicators, incorporated in contracts with external suppliers also define the buying organisation's expectations in regard to performance.

Used for the following purposes:

- To help identify the best suppliers
- To suggest how relationships with suppliers can be enhanced
- To help ensure that suppliers live up to what was promised in their contracts
- To provide suppliers with an incentive
- To significantly improve supplier performance

Benefits of using KPIs:

- Increased and improved communication on performance issues
- Motivation to achieve or surpass the specified performance level
- Support for collaborative buyer-supplier relations
- The ability directly to compare year on year performance
- Focus on key results areas
- Clearly defined shared goals
- Reduced conflict

KPIs can have some disadvantages as well. The pursuit of individual KPIs can lead to some dysfunctional or sub-optimal behaviour: cutting corners on quality or service to achieve productivity or time targets, say, or units focusing on their own targets at the expense of cross-functional collaboration and co-ordination.

Contract terms and schedules

The role of a contract is to set out the agreed roles, rights and obligations of both parties in a commercial transaction or relationship.

- **Express terms** are clearly stated and recognised in the contract between the parties (eg price, delivery dates etc).
- **Implied terms** are terms which are assumed to exist by virtue of common law and statute (for example, terms in the UK Sale of Goods Act).
- A **condition** is a vital term of the contract: if breached, the innocent party has the option of treating the contract as ended.
- A **warranty** is a less important term. The innocent party may claim damages only.

Each firm will draw up its own 'standard terms of business', and will seek to ensure that these terms are accepted by other firms with whom they deal.

For more complex and/or larger, more strategically critical purchases, it would be worth the time and expense of negotiation and drafting of contract-specific terms and conditions.

Where an organisation has recurring dealings with a supplier, or recurring requirements for a product or service, it may develop its own **standard contract**.

Model form contracts are published by third party experts, incorporating standard practice in contracting for specific purposes within specific industries, and ensuring a fair balance of contractual rights and responsibilities for buyer and seller.

Contract schedules appended to the contract cover areas such as pricing, health and safety, confidentiality, subcontractors, supplier staff.

OWN NOTES

OWN NOTES

CHAPTER 2

Legal Issues in Creating Commercial Agreements

Elements of a binding contract

Reasons why purchasers should have a working knowledge of commercial law:

- The organisation's response to the law is not 'optional' or left to managerial discretion.
- The requirements are constantly changing.
- Purchasing involves activities which are the specific focus of law and regulation.
- The common law principle is that 'ignorance of the law is no excuse'.
- If you know how complex the law is, you are more likely to seek professional advice from legal experts when you need to.

Elements of a legally binding agreement:

- Agreement, in the form of an exchange of offer and acceptance
- Consideration
- Intention to create legal relations
- Contractual capacity

The offeror must make a definite promise to be legally bound on specific terms. Not all 'statements' amount to an *offer* (eg an invitation to treat is not an offer). Once an offer has been made, the other party (the 'offeree') must **accept** the offer, clearly, unconditionally and freely.

Two main rules on consideration:

- Consideration must be valuable but need not be adequate.
- Consideration must be **sufficient** (past consideration and pre-existing obligations don't count).

In commercial contexts, there is a strong presumption that the parties intend agreements to be legally binding. However, this can be challenged.

Most individuals, and companies, have contractual capacity. On behalf of a business, owners, directors etc have contractual capacity.

In most cases, there is no requirement for a particular form of contract to be adopted. For example, it is not necessary in principle for most contracts to be in writing: oral agreements are binding, provided that the other essential elements are in place. However, it is generally preferable to put commercial agreements in writing, in order to minimise risk.

Invalid and incomplete agreements

A contract may be vitiated (flawed) by a number of factors, such as mistake, misrepresentation, duress or undue influence, or illegality. In such cases, the contract is either void or voidable.

- *Void*: having no legal effect on either party, as though no contract was ever formed.
- *Voidable*: either party can make the contract void.

A statement, written or oral, made during negotiations leading to a contract, may be understood as:

- A *term* of the subsequent contract; or merely
- A *representation* designed to 'induce' the contract.
- If a representation is included in the contract as one of its terms, and if it is then later found to be untrue, the party misled has remedies for breach of contract, as well as for misrepresentation.
- If the representation does not become a term of the contract, the party misled will have remedies only for misrepresentation.

Misrepresentation is a false statement of material fact made by one of the contracting parties, before or at the time of entering into the contract, which was intended to (and did) induce the other party to make the contract.

Mistake describes a situation in which one or more of the parties end up bound by a contact to which they did not intend to commit themselves or which turns out not to be valid.

Duress and undue influence apply if pressure is placed on one party to agree to a contract, in such a way that it does not therefore reflect the true intentions or wishes of both parties. Since one party has not freely consented to the agreement made, the contract is voidable, at the option of the coerced or influenced party.

The above principles are designed to protect a contracting party from being disadvantaged by a contract where there was no genuine agreement on terms. However, under the common law principle *caveat emptor* (Latin for 'let the buyer beware'), buyers are *not* protected in law for foolishness or negligence in making a 'bad bargain'.

Legality may also render a contract void. The courts will not uphold a contract if its purpose, intent or effect is contrary to law. Such a contract is unenforceable.

Issues in offer and acceptance

To be considered legally valid, the offer must fulfil certain requirements.

- It must be a **definite, unequivocal or unambiguous statement** of willingness to be bound in contract.

- It must be an offer that the offeror intends to be **bound by**.
- It must be **communicated successfully** to the offeree, in such a way that he is aware of it.
- It must be 'open' (still in force) when the offeree accepts it.

The offer must be 'open' (still in force) when the offeree accepts it: once an offer has been closed (if a limited time is given for response) or revoked (withdrawn by the offeror), or rejected, it can no longer be accepted.

- If the offer is stated only to be open for a specific **time period**, it will 'lapse' after the expiration of this time.
- If the offer was made subject to a **condition**, it will 'lapse' on failure of that condition.
- An offer can be **revoked** at any time before it has been accepted, even if the offeror has stated that he will keep the offer open for a stated time.
- An offer can be terminated by **rejection**.

Acceptance is an *unconditional assent* ('yes') to *all the terms of an offer*. If an offeree attempts to change the terms of the offer or qualify its effectiveness in any way, this is taken as a *rejection* of the offer and the presentation of a *counter-offer* – which must then be accepted by the other party.

A **request for further details** about an offer does *not* necessarily constitute a counter-offer.

Not all statements by a buyer or supplier amount to an 'offer' – and *only* an offer can be accepted, leading to a contract. An invitation to treat is not an offer in itself: merely an *invitation to others to make an offer*, as part of negotiation. A statement of price in answer to an enquiry is not an offer: merely a supply of information.

Standard terms of contracts

Each firm will draw up its own 'standard terms of business', and will seek to ensure that these terms are accepted by other firms with whom they deal.

Lysons & Farrington suggest a general contract structure, incorporating standard terms. This would include names and signatures of the parties; definitions; general terms; commercial provisions; secondary commercial provisions; and standard clauses.

The buyer risks contracting on disadvantageous terms, if he simply agrees to contract on the supplier's standard terms.

- He may end up with liability for risks and costs.
- He may end up with significant cost uncertainty.
- He may receive goods which are faulty, or of poor quality.
- He may be committed to paying for goods on disadvantageous payment or credit terms.
- He may lack contractual tools with which to motivate and manage supplier performance.

Legal problems may also arise if the buyer's standard terms of purchase differ from the supplier's standard terms of sale. This creates what is known as the **battle of the forms**, often 'won' by the party who 'fires the last shot'.

To avoid this:

- Send acknowledgement copies of all enquiries, accompanied by the buyer's terms, which potential suppliers must complete and return, indicating agreement.
- Send acknowledgement copies of all purchase orders, which the supplier should sign and return, indicating agreement with the buyer's terms.
- Negotiate contracts with suppliers, agreeing specific terms and conditions.
- Check any revised terms or conditions.
- Stamp delivery notes 'goods received on buyer's terms and conditions'.

The implications of international law

The fact that supply relationships increasingly take place in an international context gives rise to particular legal difficulties, in relation to issues such as: which country's law will govern the contract; and in whose courts any contractual dispute will be heard.

Many attempts have been made over the years to standardise the terms on which export and import transactions are made. Some of the common issues arising are as follows.

- When does an offer or acceptance become effective in an international trade transaction?
- When do title, property and risk in the goods sold pass from the overseas seller to the domestic buyer?
- What are the rights of a party when goods do not conform to the contract?

The **Uniform Law on Sales** defines a sale of goods as international when the parties reside or operate in different nation states and the goods are to be transported from one nation state to another, or where both offer and acceptance are made in one nation state and delivery is made in another.

Under UK law (the Uniform Law on International Sales Act 1967), a UK buyer is not compelled to adopt the Vienna Convention when buying from overseas, but if it does so, then buyer and seller accept certain obligations under the Uniform Law on Sales.

- The seller has three fundamental duties: to deliver the goods, to deliver the relevant documentation; and to transfer the property in the goods
- The buyer has two duties: to pay the price expressed in the contract of sale, and to take delivery of goods according to the terms of the contract of sale.

The complementary **Uniform Law on Formation** tries to resolve the differences between English and European law in particular, on the basic tenets of contract law: offer and acceptance. For example, under English law an offer can, in theory, always be revoked until it is accepted, while in most European countries, an offer is binding as soon as it is made. Under the Uniform Law:

- An offer can, in principle, be revoked *unless* it states a fixed time for acceptance (in which case it must stay open for at least that period), or if it specifically states that it is irrevocable, or if revocation is not made in good faith or in conformity with fair trading.

- A qualified acceptance is not an acceptance: as in English law, it constitutes a counter-offer. However, if the qualification is very minor, it is considered an acceptance.

The Rome Convention allows the parties to the contract to agree on which law will be applicable. If the applicable law is not expressed in the contract, and questions or disputes arise, it may be inferred from the nature of the contract and the prevailing circumstances. The general rule is that the choice of law should be the law with which the contract is most closely associated: generally, the law of the country in which the contractual work is to be performed.

The communication difficulties involved in international trade have long been recognised as a problem. With this in mind, the concept of incoterms (International Commercial Terms) was introduced by the International Chamber of Commerce (ICC) in 1936. It was felt that if the parties concerned in an international transaction adopted standard terms, many problem areas could be averted, as all parties would be clear on their areas of risk and responsibility at all stages of the transaction – and there would be no ambiguity of law or jurisdiction in the event of a dispute.

Incoterms is a set of contractual conditions or terms that can be adopted into international contracts, which are designed to be understood and interpreted on a worldwide basis. It sets out agreed explanations of many of the terms used in international trade to define the obligations of seller and buyer. The document is regularly updated in line with developments in commercial practice: the most recent edition being *Incoterms 2010* (effective from 1 January 2011).

There is no legal requirement to use incoterms when drawing up an international commercial contract: buyers and suppliers may contract with each other on whatever terms they think most suitable. However, if they specifically refer to an incoterm (or 'adopt' an incoterm into the contract), both parties agree to be bound by the detailed specifications laid out in *Incoterms 2010*: in the event of a dispute, the courts will 'imply' the standards of incoterms in law.

OWN NOTES

CHAPTER 3

Contractual Agreements for Supply

One-off purchases

A one-off purchase might range from:

- Low-value new purchases (or occasional re-buys), to
- The contracting of a one-off service, to
- The procurement of a high-value, long lifecycle capital asset.

A contract for a one-off purchase:

- Commits both buyer and supplier to all the terms relevant to supply of the specified requirement, in a specific case.
- *Only* commits the buyer and supplier to purchase and supply of the specified requirement, in a specific case.

Both buyer and supplier are legally bound to perform all the specific terms of the contract: to buy and supply the agreed quantity and quality of agreed goods, at the agreed time, for the agreed price. But a one-off purchase only commits the buyer and supplier to purchase and supply of that specific requirement. Both buyer and supplier are free to switch, change prices etc.

This is advantageous to the buyer where:

- There are plenty of suppliers in the market offering broadly similar goods
- Purchasing costs are low
- Price advantages can be obtained by maintaining competition.

Blanket, call-off and systems contracts

An alternative to a one-off purchase is the issue of a **standing offer**. A standing offer is where there has been a general invitation to supply a series of things as and when required. The supplier has tendered, and made an offer, to supply that ongoing requirement. Such an offer is then open to a **series of acceptances** whenever an actual order is placed under the contract. *Each acceptance completes a distinct contract.*

If a buyer does not place any orders, or places fewer orders than the full quantity originally contemplated by the tender, he is *not* in breach of contract.

One of the simplest and most common ways to handle recurring purchases is blanket ordering. This is an agreement under which a supplier undertakes to provide an estimated quantity of items over an agreed period of time at an agreed price.

When the buyer needs a delivery of the items he initiates a simplified 'release' procedure which avoids the need to go through all the stages of the traditional purchasing cycle.

Blanket ordering is appropriate for the purchase of items with low unit value, but for which there is a large, recurring requirement. A typical application for this technique is in the ordering of consumable office supplies such as stationery. Blanket ordering cuts out the staff time and paperwork that would be involved in numerous small orders, and assures regular supply.

A **call-off contract** is a term given to a contract set up between the buyer and seller where there is an overall commitment to purchase a given quantity of items or services over the period of the call-off contract. It normally operates in the same way as the 'standing offer' discussed earlier.

The term **systems contracting** is used for a broader arrangement where the buyer sets up an agreement on terms and conditions for the recurring procurement of a particular item or items.

Framework agreements

Framework agreements provide an alternative way of arranging a number of similar contracts efficiently, and are especially recommended as a contracting mechanism for public sector organisations. They are defined as: 'An agreement or other arrangement between one or more contracting authorities [buyers] and one or more economic operators [suppliers] which establishes the terms (in particular the terms as to price, and where appropriate, quality) under which the economic operator *will enter into one or more contracts* with a contracting authority in the period during which the framework agreement applies.'

In most cases, the framework is not itself a contract. The frameworks establish the basic terms and conditions that will apply to subsequent call-off orders: saving the need for *repeating* the full competitive tendering procedures for individual purchase contracts.

When a need arises for works, goods or services, the buyer has three basic options.

- To **issue call-off orders against the framework with a selected supplier**
- To **run a further mini-competition**
- To **go elsewhere**

Where a framework agreement is awarded to a **single supplier**, call-offs under the agreement can simply be awarded on the basis of the terms laid down in the agreement.

Where a framework agreement is awarded to **multiple suppliers**, there are two possible options for awarding call-offs.

- Apply the terms of the framework agreement.
- Hold a mini-competition between capable framework participants.

Services contracts

- **Goods** are tangible or material items, which can be consumed. 'Consumer goods' are items people purchase to satisfy their needs and wants: such as clothing, food and electronic goods. 'Industrial goods' or 'producer goods' refer to the inputs or resources that producers utilise, like cotton, steel, parts or subassemblies.
- **Services** are actions individuals or organisations perform which confer a benefit, but do not result in the 'ownership' of anything. Something is 'done for you', but there is no transfer of ownership of anything as part of the service transaction.
- **Works** includes projects such as the construction, alteration, repair, maintenance or demolition of buildings or structures; the installation of fittings; and so on.

Services (and service elements) present buyers with problems additional to those that arise in purchasing materials or manufactured goods, when it comes to accurate specification.

Key performance indicators (KPIs) should be drawn up to suit the needs of a particular service contract.

- Where possible, such goals will be *quantitative*.
- Some targets, however, will be more *qualitative*. For example, you may want to evaluate user satisfaction, or the effectiveness of the supplier's account management.

Service level agreements (SLAs) are formal statements of performance requirements, specifying the exact nature and level of service to be provided by a service supplier. The main purpose of a service level agreement is to define the customer's service level needs and secure the commitment of the supplier to meeting those needs.

Outsourcing is the process whereby an organisation delegates major non-core activities or functions, under contract, to specialist external service providers, potentially on a long-term relational basis. Organisations now routinely contract with specialist external suppliers to provide services such as cleaning, catering, security, facilities management, IT management, recruitment and training, accounting, legal, transport and distribution – and procurement.

Outsourcing requires a high degree of trust between buyer and contractor.

Hiring and leasing

Hiring and leasing are closely related contractual approaches, through which

- The **ownership** of an asset remains with another organisation (the bailor), but
- The customer or client organisation (the bailee) enjoys **possession and use** of the asset in exchange for payment.

Hiring is a method of renting an item from a business which exists to supply that class of item to those who wish to use it from time to time.

A **contract of hire of goods** arises where the owner of the goods merely allows the hirer to have possession of the goods for a specified period. This is *not* a contract of sale of goods, because there is no intention to transfer ownership. Hire contracts are often standard contracts, prepared on the standard terms of business of the hire organisation.

A hire contract will be particularly appropriate for short-term requirements, when it would not be cost effective to make a major capital investment in an asset only required for a short project, task or occasional need.

If the need for an asset is ongoing, a contract of **hire purchase** may be appropriate. This is a contract under which the owner of the goods (the hirer or bailor) hires them to another party, which has the *option to purchase* once all the agreed instalments have been paid.

A contract of hire purchase is also *not* a contract for the sale of goods. The hirer does not obtain immediate ownership: for the duration of the agreement, it merely has possession. It is not an 'agreement to sell', either, because the contract does *not* give the hirer a 'right' to ownership once the instalments have been paid: it merely gives it an *option* to purchase.

Leasing is a more long-term, finance-based arrangement, in which a leasing company (or 'lessor') contracts with the customer (or 'lessee') to buy an asset (from a third party) and hire it to the customer. The lessor (generally a finance company) buys and owns the asset, and the lessee pays regular instalments over a pre-determined period, to have possession and use of it.

The lessee will generally have the right to secure outright ownership from the lessor, once sufficient payments have been made under the agreement. Effectively, the lessor 'assists in the purchase' of the asset, but retains ownership of it as collateral or security for its 'loan'.

OWN NOTES

OWN NOTES

CHAPTER 4

The Role of Negotiation in Procurement and Supply

4

Commercial negotiation

Negotiation in the procurement and supply context is 'a process of planning, reviewing and analysing used by a buyer and a seller to reach acceptable agreements or compromises [which] include all aspects of the business transaction, not just price.'

In a wider context, negotiation may be defined more broadly as: 'a process whereby two parties come together to confer, in a situation in which there is some divergence or conflict of interests between them, with a view to concluding a jointly acceptable agreement.'

In this broader sense, negotiation can be seen as an **interpersonal problem-solving technique,** enabling parties to meet their own needs (as far as possible) in a conflict of interests, without damaging ongoing relations between them.

In any business relationship, a procurement professional may need to negotiate:

- What objectives will be set and given priority in making plans and managing projects
- Mutually acceptable terms and conditions of work and working together
- Approaches to conflicts and problems that may arise in the course of work.

Alternatives to negotiation:

- Competitive bidding
- Persuasion
- Giving in
- Coercion
- Problem solving

Buyer-supplier relationships may require negotiation at two levels: strategic and tactical. **Strategic negotiation** is carried out less frequently and at a higher level, usually by senior management teams from both parties. It addresses long-range issues. **Tactical negotiation** is carried out more frequently and at a lower level, usually by functional or cross-functional teams from both parties. It addresses short-range issues.

Negotiation in the sourcing process

Procurement professionals typically play one of two distinct roles in negotiation.

- Acting as the company's sole negotiator (for low-value, non-critical items) with the sales negotiator of the supplier.
- Acting as team leader of a cross-functional negotiating team (for high-value, technically complex or strategic contracts, and for the development of long-term supply relationship agreements).

Negotiation may also be used throughout a standard sourcing cycle for a given item or service.

Business needs are commonly identified via a purchase requisition from a user department, a stock-replenishment requisition from inventory control, or a new product design specification. Negotiation may be required, as a result of procurement's role in *challenging* user-identified requirements, to ensure that they are commercially sound and add value.

Specification also affects negotiation because the more 'open', or less prescriptive, the specification, the more leeway there is for the negotiating team to negotiate a total package of value: better or more innovative solutions, lower total cost of ownership, quality improvements and so on – not just 'lowest price to conform to specification'.

Negotiation may be the main approach by which a commercial agreement or purchase contract is arrived at in the private sector, or it may be used in support of tendering.

Negotiation may be necessary in situations where the terms of sale include many and varied clauses, or if the buyer suspects that the quoted price is unreasonably high.

Even if non-negotiatory competitive tendering is used, a supplier's tender may need clarification. Post-tender negotiation (PTN) may be used if there is the possibility of improvement in the supplier's offer. PTN should only be used within the ethical guidelines laid down by CIPS.

Even when a negotiation is concluded and an agreement reached buyers must still engage in contract management and relationship management over the life of the procurement.

Negotiation in conflict resolution

One of the key roles of procurement is to develop and maintain co-operative working relationships in the organisation and the supply chain. This can involve conflict management.

Conflict can be highly desirable. It can energise relationships and clarify issues. It can be a helpful aspect of negotiation, or a driver for negotiation.

Conflict can also be *destructive,* negative and damaging to relationships. Such conflict may need to be resolved or reduced, and negotiation is *one* approach to doing this.

Sources of conflict in procurement and supply:

- Interdependence and shared resources
- Differences in goals, values and perceptions
- Power imbalance
- Ambiguity

Procurement and supply may often experience **conflict with other functions**. Conflict may also arise **within the purchasing team**. Finally, conflict may arise in **relationships and interactions with suppliers**.

Negotiation in team and stakeholder management

A team has been defined as 'a small group of people with complementary skills who are committed to a common purpose, performance goals and approaches for which they hold themselves basically jointly accountable'. Teams are increasingly used in procurement and supply.

In the arena of team management and employee relations, there are three main contexts in which more or less formal negotiations may be required.

- Grievance and conflict handling
- Group problem-solving
- Negotiating terms and conditions

In addition, *informal* negotiation may be used as an operating style by a team leader, to resolve interpersonal and task-related conflicts; informally negotiate roles and task allocations; reach mutually acceptable team-based decisions; and exercise leadership.

'Stakeholders are those individuals or groups who depend on the organisation to fulfil their own goals and on whom, in turn, the organisation depends.' This includes managers and employees, supply chain partners, shareholders, bankers etc.

Stakeholders can be seen from the viewpoint of the organisation as a whole, but it is also possible to talk about the stakeholders of a project, plan or particular activity. Stakeholders in a particular commercial negotiation with an external supplier, for example, might include:

- The negotiators
- The contract managers
- The members of both organisations who will be responsible for implementing the agreement reached
- The users of the products or services supplied under the agreement
- The budget holders or financers of the procurement
- The senior management of both organisations

A buyer's responsibility is to negotiate the most effective agreement on behalf of his 'internal customers' or clients: the functions or business units benefiting from his procurement expertise, and from the users of goods, works and services. This in itself may require a negotiation process. Richard Morse identifies reasons why a failure to achieve negotiated internal agreement will cause serious problems.

- Resources will not be available.
- Implementation will falter.
- There is a risk of internal resistance or even sabotage.
- Team members will lack a common voice.
- There is a risk of alienating internal supporters.

Negotiators may need to assess the power and interest of wider stakeholders in the issue or decision, in order to determine which third-party interests they may be representing in the negotiation; whether these strengthen or weaken their bargaining position; and what outcomes may be supported or resisted by third parties.

Mendelow's power/interest matrix is a useful tool for mapping stakeholders according to their power to influence a negotiation (or other activity) and the likelihood of their showing an interest in it.

Once key stakeholders have been identified, it is possible to plan a management strategy for each. You might use a standard process, such as the following.

- Goal analysis
- Desired outcomes
- Relationship management
- Issues management
- Danger signals

OWN NOTES

OWN NOTES

CHAPTER 5

Negotiation Outcomes and Approaches

Outcomes of commercial negotiations

'Objectives' for negotiation are specific (ideally, measurable) statements of what a negotiator wants to achieve from a negotiation process: a price reduction, say, or an improvement in quality or delivery performance from a supplier. 'Outcomes' are, more broadly, the results of the negotiation process.

In most successful business negotiations, both sides win something: 'win-win negotiation'. The winnings, however, are seldom equally divided; invariably, one side wins more than the other.

Three possible outcomes:

- **Win-lose:** one party gets what he wants at the expense of the other party.
- **Lose-lose**: neither party gets what it really wants.
- **Win-win:** both parties get as close as possible to what they really want.

A classic example used to illustrate these outcomes is two men fighting over an orange.

Steele & Beasor suggest that the best outcome may in fact be a **win-perceived win**.

Orientations to negotiation

There are two basic orientations to negotiation:

- **Distributive bargaining** involves the *distribution of limited resources*, or 'dividing up a fixed pie'. The bigger one party's 'slice of the pie', the less is left for the other.
- **Integrative negotiation** involves collaborative problem-solving to *increase the options available* (or 'expanding the pie'), with the aim of exploring possibilities for both parties to find a mutually satisfying or win-win solution.

Conflict-handling styles can be mapped on two dimensions, according to the intentions of the parties involved.

- Their **assertiveness**
- Their **co-operativeness**

This analysis leads to five resulting conflict handling styles.

- **Avoiding**: you withdraw from the conflict or attempt to sweep it under the carpet.
- **Forcing/competing**: you use superior power (including bargaining power) to impose your solution on the problem.
- **Accommodating**: you concede the issue without a fight, to preserve harmony.
- **Compromising**: you make concessions to the other party, in exchange for gaining concessions (ideally of approximately equal value) from them.
- **Collaborating**: you work together to try and find an outcome which meets the clearly stated needs of both parties as far as possible.

There is no 'one best' style: negotiators need awareness and behavioural flexibility.

The dual concerns model suggests that the style of negotiation adopted will depend on the relative importance of the relationship and the substantive outcome.

It is now generally recognised that integrative or collaborative negotiation is the most constructive and sustainable approach, where the key aim is to maintain ongoing positive working relations between the parties after the negotiation. However, it is important (in business, as in exam answers) to avoid giving the impression that 'integrative is good; distributive is bad'. There is still a place for competitive bargaining.

Distributive negotiation

The key objective of distributive bargaining, as we have seen, is to maximise our party's share of value from this particular deal. Three basic strategies to achieve a 'win-lose' outcome:

- Pushing for a settlement as close as possible to the other party's resistance point
- Making the other party lower its resistance point
- Making the other party think that *this* settlement is the best it can hope to achieve

Tactics of distributive bargaining:

- Presenting exaggerated initial positions, demands or opening bids
- Exaggerating the initial distance between the two parties' positions
- Withholding information that might highlight areas of common ground or weakness
- Using all available levers to coerce, pressure or manipulate the other party
- Offering no concessions in return

Integrative negotiation

Cornelius and Faire outline a win-win approach to negotiating as follows.

Step 1 Be willing to create a free exchange of information.
Step 2 Find out *why* each party needs what they say they want.
Step 3 Find out where the interests of both parties dovetail.
Step 4 Design new options, where everyone gets more of what they need.
Step 5 Co-operate. Treat the other person as a partner, not an opponent.

Typical integrative tactics reflect a 'pull' influencing approach, in which the aim is to align the interests of both parties.

- Being open about your own needs and concerns in the situation, and seeking to understand those of the other party: getting all cards on the table
- Collaboratively generating options
- Focusing on areas of common ground and mutual benefit
- Supporting the other party in accepting your proposals
- Maintaining and modelling flexibility

Characteristics of effective integrative negotiators:

- Excellent listening skills
- A holistic or systemic orientation
- Abundance or added-value thinking
- Maturity and assertiveness
- Integrity and trust
- Emotional intelligence

Principled negotiation

Negotiation has traditionally depended on **positional bargaining**: each side takes a 'position' on an issue, arguing in its favour and attempting to get an outcome as close to that initial position as possible. The focus on positions fosters a win-lose or lose-lose outcome.

In contrast, *principled* negotiation sees the parties as working collaboratively to attack a shared problem or to maximise a shared opportunity. Fisher and Ury advocate a style that is both hard on the problem *and* soft on the people.

Principled negotiation is also identified as a way of *shifting* negotiations from a distributive towards a more integrative approach.

Principled negotiation requires:

- Separating the people from the problem
- Focusing on reconciling interests
- Generating a variety of ideas and options
- Insisting that the agreement reflect some objectively fair standard.

Developing target outcomes for negotiation

A simple approach to setting objectives is given by the acronym MIL, originally coined by Gavin Kennedy. Kennedy distinguishes between objectives we Must achieve, objectives we Intend to achieve (or which it is Important for us to achieve), and objectives we would Like to achieve.

- **Must-achieve objectives** are potential deal-breakers.
- **Intend-to-achieve objectives** represent a target of negotiation, but failure to achieve one or more of them will not necessarily be disastrous.

- **Like-to-achieve objectives** are just 'icing on the cake'.

More terminology:

- **Limits** also called **resistance points** (the point beyond which a negotiator will not be pushed) or **walkaway points** (the point at which it is a better option to walk away from the negotiation than to make further concessions to complete it).
- **Target points** are the points you realistically expect to achieve in a settlement.
- **Alternatives** are other deals negotiators could achieve and still meet their needs.

Negotiations with suppliers have traditionally been carried out by means of a win-lose approach. There is a risk here that, even if the buyer is successful in 'winning' the negotiation, the process could damage the supplier's commitment, the buyer's status or reputation as a good customer, and the long-term buyer-supplier relationship – all of which could lead to damaging consequences at a later date.

Lysons & Farrington point out, concisely, that: 'The only reason we negotiate is to produce something better than the results we could obtain *without* negotiating.' A 'successful negotiation' or 'unsuccessful negotiation' is often defined by whether a deal has been 'completed' or not. In fact, the more important measure may be – *not* whether the negotiator has 'completed an agreement' or 'reached a deal' – but whether he has *made wise choices* in the best interests of his firm and relevant stakeholders.

In some circumstances, the optimal solution may be to 'walk away'. Having a Plan B or back-up plan (the BATNA), as an acceptable alternative to a negotiated agreement:

- Enables you to be more assertive during negotiation
- Protects you from feeling that you 'have to' accept terms that are too unfavourable
- Provides a decision rule

OWN NOTES

5

OWN NOTES

CHAPTER 6

Power and Relationships

Power and influence in commercial negotiation

Power is the ability of an individual or group to exercise influence over others. Power is not the same as 'authority', which refers to the scope and amount of discretion given to a person to make decisions by virtue of the position he holds in an organisation.

A negotiator may have delegated authority to negotiate on behalf of his organisation, and to exercise authority as leader of a procurement team, say. However, a buyer does *not* have formal positional authority over a supplier or other external negotiating party.

If one party to the negotiation has greater power than the other, there is an opportunity to apply **leverage**.

The judicious use of power is essential in negotiation in order to:

- Secure a 'win' outcome for one's own party
- Maximise one's own party's share of value gains
- Move the negotiating process forward
- Push through negotiating barriers
- Secure agreement, commitment and buy-in.

Power in buyer-supplier relationships.

- **Overt power** is obvious, or transparent – through direct tactics.
- **Covert power** is subtle, hidden or implied – through indirect tactics.
- **Structural power** (*Cox*) is built into the situation, context or relationship.

Coercive, arbitrary, unfair or abusive exercise of power in supplier relations is to be discouraged.

Sources of power and leverage

French and Raven: five sources of power in organisational relationships

- Legitimate power (or position power)
- Expert power
- Reward power (or 'resource power')
- Referent power (or 'personal power')
- Coercive power (or physical power)

An individual can operate from any or all of these bases of power, according to which one is appropriate, effective and relevant in a particular relationship. Purchasers are perhaps most likely to exercise **reward power** in relation to suppliers, with the ability to award contracts and/or follow-on business.

Lewicki *et al* identify a wide range of sources of power (slightly differently classified) that can specifically be applied in negotiation situations: informational; personality and individual differences; position-based; relationship-based; and contextual power.

One of the most important steps in preparing for a negotiation is to appraise the relative power (or bargaining strength) of the two parties: in this case, the buyer and the supplier. It's important for the exam to know the situations when the bargaining power of buyers is likely to be high, and similarly for suppliers.

The power and dependency model of Cox *et al:* where B is important to A, but A is not important to B, then B is the dominant partner in the relationship. Independence (neither party needs the relationship) and interdependence (both parties need the relationship) create a more equal balance of power. Broadly speaking, each party will wish to avoid a situation where the other party is dominant.

Buyers can use the power/dependency model in two ways.
* To determine the most effective negotiating approach
* To attempt to create new power circumstances that provide for a more congenial leverage position

Improving leverage:
* Increasing expert and informational power
* Increasing resource power
* Increasing legitimate power
* Manipulating structural factors in buyer-supplier power
* Using effective persuasion methods and influencing techniques

The relationship context

Commercial relationships may vary widely in the extent of their intensity, mutuality, trust and commitment – in other words, their 'closeness'. Writers often refer to a relationship 'spectrum' extending from one-off arm's length transactions at one end to long-term collaborative partnerships at the other.

At the closer, more relational end of the spectrum, more complex and wide-ranging negotiations will be required to secure ongoing, flexible, value-adding collaboration. At the more distant, transactional end of the spectrum, little negotiation may be used.

Characteristics of adversarial relationships:
* Lack of trust and therefore little information sharing

- A one-off or short-term transaction focus
- The use of power and negotiation to seek the best possible deal
- Rigorously enforced compliance with contract terms
- Little co-operation or recognition of mutual interests

These relationships are 'transactional' rather than 'relational'.

In collaborative relationships, the parties intentionally seek to develop long-term, mutually beneficial ongoing dealings. The strategic view is that both buyer and supplier share common interests, and both can benefit from seeking ways to add value in the supply chain: 'enlarging the pie' offers a win-win situation, where buyer, supplier and end-customer can all benefit.

Features of a constructive supply partnership:

- Joint and mutual search for greater efficiency and competitiveness
- Joint planning for the future by the customer and the supplier
- Agreed shared objectives
- A joint effort to eliminate waste from the supply chain
- Openness and transparency between the organisations
- Each party understands the expectations of the other
- The relationship is one of equal partners
- A prepared and agreed exit strategy

What kind of relationship is best?

Factors affecting the most appropriate relationship type for a given purchasing situation:

- The nature and importance of the items being purchased
- The competence, capability, co-operation and performance of the supplier
- Geographical distance
- The compatibility of the supply partners
- The organisation's and purchasing function's objectives and priorities
- Supply market conditions

Arguments for a transactional approach:

- A more adversarial approach to negotiation may well secure the best commercial deal.
- Developing collaborative relationships takes time and effort.
- There are risks in long-term relationships.

Drivers for collaborative relationships:

- Whole supply chains – not individual firms – compete in the global marketplace.
- Organisations are increasingly outsourcing non-core activities.
- ICT developments have enabled and supported networking and relationships.
- There is pressure for companies to protect and leverage their intellectual property.
- Transactional approach fails to leverage competitive and value-adding potential.
- There are costs of adversarial relationships.
- Closer relationships and integration help to reduce waste in supply chains.

An organisation may need to develop a *portfolio* of relationships.

- The organisation might **focus relationship investment** on the 20% of suppliers who provide 80% of total supply value.
- The organisation may use a blend of approaches: an **adversarial-collaborative** approach, for example.

Kraljic's matrix is one way of classifying supplies and suppliers and deciding on the best relationship in each case. The two key factors are the importance of the procurement and the complexity of the supply market.

The supplier preferencing model shows how suppliers rate buyers in terms of their inherent attractiveness and the value of their business.

Building and maintaining positive relationships

Relationship drivers are key qualities or values which build constructive relationships.

- **Quality of interaction**.
- **Trust** is central to the success of supply chain relationships.
- **Transparency** is the willingness to share information.
- **Commitment** is the intention or desire of one or both parties to continue in a relationship, and to invest in maintaining it.
- **Co-operation and collaboration** foster relationships.
- **Mutuality, exchange or reciprocity** are all terms to express the idea that both parties gain some benefit from the relationship.

Trust means having confidence in the truthfulness, integrity, competence and reliability of another person or party – and acting accordingly (eg by proceeding with your own part in a negotiated agreement on the basis that they will do what they have said they will do). Trust is a crucial pre-condition for open, honest communication – which in turn is the basis for positive and deepening collaborative relationships.

Five key elements to developing high-trust supplier relationships:

- Model the behaviours you expect.
- Keep and exceed commitments.
- Proactively develop trust, and measure trust development.
- Disclose information.
- Be empathetic.

Key ethical issues in negotiation and supplier relationship management:

- The provision of fair, truthful and accurate (not false or misleading) information
- The confidentiality of information, where appropriate
- Fair dealing with supply chain partners
- Avoidance of conflicts of interest
- Equitable access to opportunity
- Fair trade pricing

Repairing damaged relationships

A number of intrinsic and extrinsic factors may hinder the progressive development of a commercial relationship, or actively damage it. This topic is relevant to negotiation because:

- Negotiation may be one of the **approaches used to repair relationship damage**
- Negotiation may be one of the **causes of relationship damage**.

Approaches to the management of conflict:

- Problem-solving
- Over-arching goals
- Expansion of resources
- Avoidance or smoothing
- Compromise
- Altering the human variable
- Altering the structural variable

Two approaches to relationship repair and dispute resolution:

- Issues management
- Negotiation

Alternative dispute resolution:

- Conciliation
- Mediation

Relationships can be damaged not just by conflicts or contractual disputes (which are susceptible to problem-solving and resolution): there may be lingering loss of trust due to broken promises – or due to a 'bruising' negotiation, in which one party feels coerced, disrespected or unfairly treated. Trust may therefore need to be rebuilt.

OWN NOTES

CHAPTER 7

Cost and Price Analysis

How suppliers set their prices

There are many external factors and internal factors that affect suppliers' pricing decisions. It's important for the exam to be able to describe and discuss them.

Suppliers' pricing strategies are likely to be based on either (a) costs or (b) market factors.

Cost-based pricing allows the supplier to cover its costs and make a profit.

- Full-cost pricing
- Cost-plus or mark-up pricing
- Marginal pricing
- Rate of return or 'target return' pricing
- Contribution pricing

Cost-based pricing approaches are limited in various ways.

- They ignore competition and other influences on pricing.
- They are quite inflexible.
- They do not give the supplier an incentive to reduce or manage costs.
- The supplier may be ignoring potential profits.

So in practice suppliers usually use market pricing.

- Price volume
- Market share pricing (or penetration pricing)
- Market skimming
- Current revenue pricing (or contribution pricing)
- Promotional pricing
- Market segment pricing (also called differential pricing or price discrimination
- Competition pricing (or dynamic pricing)

Factors in buyers' decisions on price:

- The buying organisation's relative bargaining power
- The number of suppliers in the market and the possibility of substitute products
- The type of purchase
- The prices paid by competitors
- The total package of benefits offered for the price
- What the buyer can afford

- What is a 'reasonable' price, based on price analysis
- What is a 'fair' (ethical and sustainable) price

Often a buyer will use price analysis or cost analysis or both.

Understanding costs

Price is what a seller charges for a package of benefits offered to a buyer. Cost is what the buying organisation pays to acquire and utilise the goods purchased.

There are three major areas in which a manufacturing business incurs costs.

- Raw materials
- Labour
- Overheads

Direct and indirect costs:

- **Direct costs** are costs which can be directly identified with a specific saleable unit of output.
- **Indirect costs (or overheads)** are expenditures on labour, materials or other items which cannot be identified with a specific saleable unit of output.

Direct costs plus production overheads = total production costs. Add on non-production overheads and we arrive at total costs.

Cost behaviour is the way in which the costs of output are affected by fluctuations in the level of activity: the volume of production, say, or the level of sales.

- Some costs do not vary as the volume of sales or production increases: a **fixed cost**.
- Some costs vary as the volume of sales or production changes: a **variable cost**.

The supplier's sales force will always be seeking to generate at least enough business to cover fixed costs: the costs incurred by the business whether they produce anything or not. If the cost structure of the supplier includes a high proportion of fixed costs, there will be strong pressure to achieve high sales volume – and this may result in competitive, incentive-level pricing. In negotiation, buyers may be able to take advantage of the seller's eagerness to do business.

Understanding fixed and variable costs can help buyers in various ways.

Some costs include a mix of fixed and variable elements. In these cases, it is necessary to determine the amount of the fixed element included in the mixed cost. A common technique for achieving this is the **high-low method**. This is based on looking at the total cost at a time when activity is at a *high* level and comparing it with the total cost at a time when activity is *low*.

In a close, long-term supply relationship, there may be a policy of:

- **Open book costing**, where suppliers provide information about their costs to buyers
- **Cost transparency**, where both buyer and supplier share cost information.

If buyers can ascertain the supplier's cost structure, the information will be useful in several ways. The buyer can assess whether the level of profit targeted by the supplier is excessive: if it is, there is scope for price reduction. Buyers can also:

- Estimate the level of sales the supplier must achieve to break even
- Compare the level of profit targeted by the supplier with that earned by competitors
- Estimate how valuable the business or contract will be to the supplier
- Estimate the lowest possible price the supplier can sustainably afford to charge.

Costing methods

There are two main approaches that may be adopted in calculating the costs of operations and products or services, whether for a supplier, or for the buying organisation.

- A **marginal (or variable) costing** approach uses only the 'marginal cost' of producing additional units: basically, using only *variable costs* to derive a unit cost.
- An **absorption costing** approach attempts to calculate the *total cost* of producing products. In addition to variable cost, a 'fair' proportion of fixed costs is allocated to (or 'absorbed into') each unit of output, as a fixed cost per unit – and to this total, a mark-up is added for profit.

Marginal costing principles are widely used in decision-making by managers. The useful distinction between variable costs (which will change under various decision alternatives) and fixed costs (which may not change) is preferable to the approach of absorption costing, in which fixed and variable costs are all aggregated in the cost of units. Another way of putting this is to say that variable costs are always **relevant costs** in terms of decision making, whereas fixed costs frequently are not relevant (because they won't change anyway).

The challenge with absorption costing is to attribute a 'fair' amount of fixed cost to each unit of production output. Traditionally, this has been done by determining the amount of some measurable resource consumed in a production period (say, labour or machine hours) and the overhead cost of that resource (eg total fixed overhead costs *divided by* labour or machine hours = overhead absorption rate per hour).

This is far from being an exact science and inaccuracy is more important nowadays, because indirect costs are typically much higher than in earlier periods. To address this, accountants have developed a more accurate approach known as **activity based costing**. This is based on the identification of cost drivers and cost pools.

There is a vital difference between the purchase price of an article and its **total cost of ownership**. Total cost of ownership includes not just the price of the items being purchased, but also: transaction costs; finance costs; acquisition costs; operating costs (eg energy use); costs of storage and handling; costs of quality; end of life costs.

'Best value' may therefore be defined as the lowest whole life cost which meets the purchaser's complex package of requirements (for quality, service, ongoing partnership with the supplier and so on) – and it is *this* total cost/benefit package that must be defined and negotiated with suppliers, for complex procurements.

Understanding profit and contribution

Profit is the difference between the selling price of a product (or the total revenue earned from selling a product) and the cost of producing the product. In other words, it is the gain or surplus left over after the manufacturer (or service provider) has paid all its costs. Profitability is the primary objective of most businesses in the private sector.

Reasons for wanting a profit:

- Profit means that the business has covered its costs – important for survival.
- Profit encourages owners to maintain their investment.
- Retained profits are available for reinvestment in the development of the business.

It is often convenient to indicate the profitability of a particular business, or a particular product, by expressing the profit as a percentage. We may choose to express the profit as a percentage of total costs, or as a percentage of selling price.

- When we express the profit element as a percentage of cost, we refer to it as a *mark-up*.
- When we express the profit as a percentage of selling price, we refer to it as a *margin*.

Contribution is the difference between sales revenue and the *variable cost* of sales. Another way of putting this is to say that it is the amount of selling price left over after variable costs have been paid for.

Changes in volume of output and sales therefore *affect costs* – and hence affect profits. **Breakeven point** is the point at which a supplier sells a sufficient volume of product to cover its costs exactly: it 'breaks even', neither making a loss nor a profit. Any additional sales will tip the balance over into profit.

If asked to calculate a breakeven point from data given, the simplest way is to plug the data into the following simple cost-volume-profit formula.

$$\text{Breakeven point (in units)} = \frac{\text{Fixed costs}}{\text{Selling price } minus \text{ variable cost per unit}}$$

You can then multiply this number of units by selling price (per unit) to get a breakeven point in sales revenue terms.

The margin of safety is the difference between the planned sales level and the breakeven sales level. The margin of safety is often expressed as a percentage of the planned sales.

Breakeven analysis has some important implications for buyers in negotiation.

- Suppliers will be conscious of the **need to reach breakeven point**, and their sales staff will be under pressure to obtain sufficient business to reach the required sales volume.
- Once a supplier has passed breakeven point, every additional unit produced and sold **represents profit**.

Negotiating prices

Negotiation and agreement on price may include a range of matters.

- The type of pricing arrangement
- The price or fee schedules
- Costs and charges incurred by the supplier in the course of the contract which are to be reimbursed by the buyer
- Contract price adjustment (CPA)
- Available discounts
- Terms of payment and credit

Price arrangements or agreements in contracts are basically of three types.

- **Fixed price agreements**, in which a schedule of fixed fees or payments is agreed in advance (and the supplier therefore bears all the risk of cost variances). More flexible variants, in supply markets with volatile labour or material costs, may include CPA clauses, price review or re-determination clauses, or level of effort term contracts.
- **Incentivised contracts** of various kinds, such as bonus payments or formulae for sharing cost savings.
- **Cost-plus agreements**, in which the buyer agrees to reimburse the supplier for all allowable, allocable and reasonable costs incurred in performing the contract, in addition to an agreed profit percentage.

Fixed price agreements are advantageous to the buyer, in terms of:

- Financial risk.
- Cashflow management
- Supplier motivation
- Administrative simplicity and contract management costs.

Cost-plus arrangements are correspondingly *disadvantageous* to the buyer, and advantageous to the supplier. There are advantages for the buyer, however, in that the final cost may be less than a fixed price contract, because the supplier does not have to quote or negotiate an inflated price in order to cover its cost-related risks.

OWN NOTES

CHAPTER 8

Economic Factors

The economic environment

The macro-economic environment embraces the general level of activity and growth in the economic system, and the effect of economic 'boom and bust' cycles. Making informed judgements and assumptions about future macro-economic events is crucially important for planning business strategy.

Here are some sources of macro-economic data to support negotiation.

- Forecasts, reports and statistical surveys published by the government
- Analysis published in the mainstream and financial media and websites
- Data published by financial institutions and analysts
- Data published by the financial markets and commodity markets and exchanges
- Published economic indices such as the retail price index (RPI)
- The websites and information services of organisations promoting trade and exports
- Online macro-economic analysis, in the form of searchable databases and reports

Organisations also operate within the more immediate economic environment of a business sector, industry and market. Product markets are the markets in which a firm sells its products and services to consumers. Supply (or factor) markets are the markets in which a firm purchases the resources it needs for production (eg materials and labour).

Two key micro-economic concepts:

- The so-called **market mechanism** is the relationship between demand and supply, and the way in which price affects both.
- The concept of **market structure** refers to the degree of competition that exists in the market for a product, and the different 'types' of markets that arise.

Purchasing research is 'the systematic study of all relevant factors which may affect the acquisition of goods and services, for the purpose of securing current and future requirements in such a way that the competitive position of the company is enhanced' (van Weele). In relation to a particular sourcing exercise or up-coming supply negotiation, the focus of purchasing research should include three basic aspects.

- Demand analysis
- Vendor analysis
- Supply market analysis

Sources of information on micro-economic factors: primary data include communication with suppliers, the buyer's own database, marketing communications from suppliers and competitors, online market exchanges, advisory and information services, trade fairs, and informal networking. There are also many sources of secondary data.

The market mechanism

Demand is the quantity of goods that customers are willing and able to buy. It varies with price: in general, as the price of a good goes up, demand goes down – because some people will cut down on their purchases, or switch to cheaper substitutes.

Factors influencing demand:

- The price of substitute goods
- The price of complementary goods
- Disposable income
- Consumer preferences and attitudes

Supply is the amount that firms are willing and able to sell. This too varies with price: in general, as the market price of a good rises, supply also rises – because higher prices mean greater profitability, increasing the willingness of firms to produce more.

Factors influencing supply:

- Production costs
- Technology
- The number of suppliers in the market
- Expectations, eg about the economic future or the level of demand

There is one price (called the 'equilibrium price') at which producers wish to sell the same amount as customers wish to buy: in other words, the market 'clears' (without either surplus supply or unsatisfied demand).

Changes in price affect demand – but this effect varies, depending on the product and market conditions. The term **price elasticity of demand** is used to describe the sensitivity of demand to changes in price. The more elastic demand is, the more demand will *increase* if you *lower* the price, and the more demand will *decrease* if you *raise* the price.

Elasticity is measured as: $\dfrac{\text{\% change in quantity demanded}}{\text{\% change in price}}$

- When elasticity is greater than 1 (elastic), a change in price will lead to significant changes in the seller's total revenue.
- When elasticity is less than 1 (inelastic), changes in prices will have much less effect on demand – causing a different set of effects on sales revenue.

In general terms, therefore, the less elastic the demand, the more it pays the organisation to raise its prices – and the more elastic the demand, the more it pays the organisation to lower its prices.

Market structure

The term 'market structure' refers to different *forms of competition* that might be found in a market. The nature and intensity of that competition will influence the behaviour and performance of the players in the market – and their pricing strategies.

There are four basic market structures.

- Perfect competition
- Monopoly
- Monopolistic competition
- Oligopoly

The situations in the middle of the spectrum (monopolistic competition and oligopoly) are sometimes referred to collectively as **imperfect competition.**

Market conditions for perfect competition:

- There are many buyers and sellers, each of them a 'price taker'.
- The goods being marketed are 'homogeneous': in other words, identical.
- 'Perfect information' about the market is available to all parties.
- There is no 'economic friction'.
- There are no 'barriers to entry or exit'.
- There is 'perfect mobility'.

Perfect competition means that there will be literally nothing to choose between one supplier and another. There is a strong incentive for suppliers to compete on price.

Market conditions for monopoly:

- Only one supplier of the good exists.
- There are barriers to entry.
- There are no close substitutes for the good being produced.

If these conditions are met, the monopolist essentially controls supply, and has absolute power to determine the price of the good in its market: it is said to be a *price maker.* Control over supply and price enables monopolists to achieve and sustain abnormal profits.

The main concern for buyers will be a *monopoly supplier*'s absolute power in the market: there will be no opportunity for the buyer to take its business elsewhere, so the monopolist will be able to dictate terms and conditions of trade.

Conditions for 'monopolistic competition':

- There are many suppliers (though not as many as in perfect competition)
- Goods are *not* homogeneous
- There are barriers to entry

Buyers will need to have a clear idea of what price and non-price criteria are most important for a given purchase category in a given set of circumstances.

An oligopoly is a situation in which a small number of large producers dominate a market in which products are differentiated. This creates a distinctive tactical climate.

- There is **little price competition** in the market.
- Competition often takes **non-price** forms.
- **Market prices** tend to be set by non-competitive means, in order to maintain price stability and avoid damaging price wars.

In an oligopoly supply market, suppliers have strong market power by virtue of their size and small number – and any type of formal or informal collusion will add to their bargaining strength and reduce that of buyers. As with a monopoly, oligopoly suppliers can therefore charge high prices.

Competition

The concept of market structure goes some way to explaining why some market types are more competitive than others, and what form that competition takes (eg price or non-price competition). However, there is another key micro-economic model which addresses the competitive forces in industries and markets, including the balance of supplier and buyer power: Porter's Five Forces Model.

- **Potential new entrants** to an industry may make it more competitive by: expanding supply (without necessarily increasing market demand). They may be deterred by barriers to entry.
- **Substitute products** are alternative products that serve the same purpose, making it easy for buyers to switch.
- **Buyer power** may make an industry more competitive by enabling buyers to: force down prices, or bargain for higher quality or improved services.
- **Supplier power** is generally exercised to raise prices in the market.
- The **intensity of rivalry** among current competitors may range from collusion between competitors to the other extreme of aggressive competitive strategies such as innovation, price wars and promotional battles.

Macro-economic factors

Macro-economic factors affect procurement – and negotiations – in a number of ways.

- The overall amount of **economic activity** determines the wealth of a nation, which influences the amount of disposable income its citizens have to spend – which in turn influences the demand for goods and services.
- Economic variables determine the strength of an economy and the extent of business confidence in it, which in turn influences the amount people are willing to invest. This may take the form of **business cycles** – which again affect demand and prices.
- **Employment and unemployment levels** may affect the availability of labour and labour costs (for suppliers and buyers), as well as disposable incomes and demand.
- **Rates of inflation** affect prices, and therefore the supplier's costs and pricing.
- The overall rate of **taxation** affects the level of demand in an economy.

- **Exchange rate fluctuations** create risk in international sourcing.
- **Interest rate fluctuations** create risk for corporate finance.

The business cycle (or trade cycle) is the periodic fluctuation in levels of economic activity, output and employment: from 'boom' to 'bust' (and back again). There are four main phases in a typical business cycle: depression; recovery; boom; and recession.

Purchasers may need to anticipate and adapt resourcing decisions and negotiations to suit each stage of the cycle.

- Investment, purchasing and inventory decisions should be tailored to the anticipated level of demand (lower in a downturn and recession, and higher again in recovery).
- Costs may need to be reduced (eg through applying negotiation leverage) to cope with recessionary phases.
- Recruitment may need to be suspended in advance of recession.

In a period of recession and financial instability (such as the 'global financial crisis' that began in 2008) economic and market analysis in preparation for negotiation will have to take account of factors such as the following.

- Understanding buyer and supplier perspectives on costs and breakeven
- Understanding pressures on profit margins
- Sustainable and ethical negotiation
- Pressures for purchasing negotiators to deliver value or low price
- The need to negotiate terms to support suppliers in financial difficulty
- The need to negotiate terms to mitigate the risk of supplier or buyer failure
- Negotiating integratively and/or ethically

Exchange rates are important for firms in international product or supply markets.

- *Importers* want to agree prices when the value of their currency is as *high* as possible.
- *Exporters* want to agree prices when the value of their currency is as *low* as possible.

Fluctuations in foreign exchange rates therefore represent a source of financial *risk*.

8

OWN NOTES

CHAPTER 9

Objectives and Variables

Defining issues and variables

There are five key questions in preparing for a negotiation.

- **What do we want?** The total package of issues for discussion is sometimes known as the **bargaining mix.**
- **How valuable is each of our 'wants' to us?** In other words, what is the relative priority of the issues and objectives, if we can't get our way on them all?
- **Why do we want what we want?** It is important to seek to understand the needs, business requirements, drivers, stakeholder influences and risks or fears *underlying* negotiation objectives on both sides.
- **What is our entry point?** This question refers to the starting point of the negotiation.
- **What is our exit point?** In other words, what is our 'walk away' position?

In one use of the term, 'variables' are essentially the 'content issues' for negotiation, which determine its scope and focus. A wide range of issues may be the focus of a negotiation process, depending on the situation. Some variables will only emerge during negotiation. Examples of possible variables include price, delivery and contractual terms.

In a related use of the term, 'variables' are the 'currencies' (tokens of value) that will be traded or exchanged in the negotiation bargaining or moving phase.

- What does your party have to offer that will be valued by the other party (and will therefore attract a valuable offer in exchange)?
- What can you offer that will be valuable for the other party to receive (eg a high priority in their objective list), while not costing you very much to give?
- What does the other party have to offer you, that you want? What value or priority do you place on this, and what would you be willing to trade in return for it?

The term 'bargaining mix' is used to describe the total package of issues (and related currencies) on the agenda for a given negotiation. A large bargaining mix – a list of lots of items for discussion – can make negotiations lengthy and complex. However, a large bargaining mix allows more possible groupings and trade-offs between issues – making it more likely that the final agreement will meet both parties' needs.

- Prioritise the issues within the bargaining mix.
- Determine which issues are connected and which are separate.

Setting objectives for negotiation

Objectives are **targets** for negotiation outcomes, clearly defining the point at which the negotiator will be satisfied and ready to move to agreement – and representing the yardstick by which the success of the negotiation will be measured. Effective objectives for negotiation have the following characteristics.

- **Specific** (clear and well defined) and ideally **measurable**
- **Acceptable**: taking into account the interests of key stakeholders
- **Realistic** or attainable
- **Tentative** or provisional

This is our negotiation-specific adaptation of the 'SMART' acronym often identified with the setting of performance measures and objectives.

In an integrative negotiation, however, effective objectives might also be:

- Flexible
- 'Chunked up
- Relational.

A three-point range of objectives: (a) a maximum or best-case position; (b) a minimum acceptable or worst-case position (below which you terminate the negotiation and resort to your BATNA); and (c) an objective, realistic or most likely position (target).

Ideally, it will be possible to determine one's own best and worst acceptable outcomes, and anticipate those of the other party. Where the two acceptable ranges overlap, there is scope for negotiation.

Negotiators can make provisional decisions on issues such as the following.

- What concessions can be made and what value is given to those concessions
- What issues or variables can be linked together (eg price and quality)
- How the other party is likely to respond to, or attempt to counter, tactics
- What tactics the other party is likely to adopt, and how they can be countered

Positions and interests

Important to distinguish between positions and interests, especially in integrative bargaining.

- **Positions** are represented by the 'stance' of the parties in negotiation: their opening bid, target point or negotiation objective.
- **Interests** are the underlying values, needs, wants and concerns that explain *why* each party wants what it wants.

The other party may not be able to accept our *position* (which will probably be in conflict with its own), but may be able to see constructive ways of meeting our *interests*.

Positional bargaining tends to be unsatisfactory at best: 'Any agreement reached may reflect a mechanical splitting of the difference between final positions rather than a solution carefully crafted to meet the legitimate interests of the parties.' At worst, it can lead to a time-consuming and relationship-damaging adversarial process.

Lewicki *et al* note that parties in conflict base their strategies on one of three things.

- **Interests**: what they need, desire or want.
- **Rights**: who is 'right' or correct, who has legitimacy, or what is fair.
- **Power**: who can exercise most influence, by dominance, economic pressures, expertise, legitimate authority and so on.

Lewicki points out that there may be many different interests at work in a negotiation.

- Substantive interests
- Process interests
- Relationship interests
- Interests in principle

Openings and presenting issues

In a distributive negotiation, there is often a clear statement of an opening bid or opening position, usually stated as the 'best possible outcome' or 'ideal solution' for the party making the first move. It is generally accepted that this will be ambitious or exaggerated – allowing room for downward movement during negotiation.

'Substantial psychological research suggests that, more often than not, negotiators who make first offers come out ahead... Making a first offer is related to one's confidence and sense of control at the bargaining table.'

However, making the first offer may not be advantageous when the other side has more information about the item under negotiation, or the supply market context.

In an integrative negotiation, the opening focus will be on collaboratively identifying and defining the 'presenting issue': the issue, problem or area of conflict that has most obviously brought the two parties to the negotiating table.

Elements involved in the definition of presenting issues:

- Define the problem in a way that is mutually acceptable to both sides.
- State the problem with an eye toward practicality and comprehensiveness.
- State the problem as a goal and identify the obstacles to attaining this goal.
- Depersonalise the problem.
- Separate the problem definition from the search for solutions.
- Seek to *understand* the problem, by reference to the underlying interests and needs of each party.

The nature of 'presenting issues' is that they may not be the *actual* or underlying issue: merely the most obvious or immediate issue which has brought the parties to the negotiating table.

Protocols and process issues

A number of process issues (elements of protocol, ground rules or order for the negotiation) may be planned in advance, either unilaterally (for discussion in the opening phase of negotiation) or, ideally, collaboratively. Lewicki *et al* identify the following protocol issues.

- What agenda should be followed?
- Where will the negotiation be held?
- How long will the negotiation take?
- What agents, observers or advisers will be involved in the negotiation?
- What might be done if negotiation fails?
- How will we keep track of what is agreed?
- How do we know whether we have a good agreement?

Lysons & Farrington similarly identify the need to prepare for issues such as:

- The order in which the issues to be negotiated should be dealt with.
- Whether to build in recesses (or 'breaks') for discussion amongst the negotiating team.

OWN NOTES

9

OWN NOTES

CHAPTER 10

Resourcing the Process

Resources for negotiation

Six main resources required to support a negotiation.

- **Personnel**. Sufficient staff, with the right experience and skills, must be available for all stages of the negotiation.
- **Finance**. There must be an adequate budget for the essential costs that will be incurred.
- **Time**. Sufficient and appropriate time must be set aside for the negotiation meeting or series of meetings.
- **Information**. Information – about the supplier, the market, environmental factors, bargaining positions and so on – is a key resource for negotiation.
- **Space and facilities**, if the negotiation is to be conducted via a face-to-face meeting in a chosen venue.
- **Information and communication technology (ICT) resources**

Decisions about the deployment of these resources in the negotiation process should take two basic considerations into account.

- The resources required to **achieve desired negotiation outcomes**
- The **opportunities for conditioning** arising from the deployment of resources. 'Conditioning' means psychologically preparing the other party to be open to persuasion: putting them in an appropriate frame of mind for the negotiating approach you intend to use.

The venue

In negotiation, as in sport, there is considered to be a 'home advantage': a psychological advantage to the party negotiating on its own turf. This advantage may arise from any or all of the following.

- Familiarity with the surroundings, facility, culture, creating a psychological 'comfort zone' and confidence which the 'away' party may lack
- Accessibility of additional resources which may be difficult for an 'away' party to carry with them
- The immediate presence of support networks
- The sense of obligation that an 'away' party may feel

Lysons & Farrington argue that: 'Buyers should normally expect the vendor to come to them, unless there are good reasons to do otherwise.'

Steele notes that it may be advantageous to negotiate at a vendor's premises as a reality check on extravagant claims of stock availability, the excellence of production facilities or the positive morale of staff. In addition, the way you are treated as a guest or visitor may provide useful information about how the supplier views you and your business.

A relatively comfortable (but business-like and professional) work environment is conducive to agreement.

More specifically, thought may be given to matters such as:

- Seating arrangements and room layout
- Access to information and communication facilities
- The 'tone' set by the venue
- The tidiness, comfort and quality of the room, furniture and facilities
- The size of the room, and the number of people it comfortably accommodates
- The availability of break-out rooms
- The availability of rest rooms and refreshments.

The participants

Negotiations may be conducted by individual representatives of each party, or by teams representing each organisation.

The majority of straight and modified re-buy procurements are likely to be negotiated on a one-to-one basis, by a buyer, contract manager or vendor manager on one side, and a sales representative, contract manager or account manager on the other.

In terms of resourcing, perhaps the key requirement for individual negotiations is that both individuals have the **authority** to negotiate and make agreements on behalf of their firms or stakeholders – ideally, *without* having constantly to refer proposals upwards to higher authority.

Lysons & Farrington suggest that: 'for important negotiations, especially where complicated technical, legal, financial and other issues are involved, or for new buy or capital purchases, a team approach is usual – as an individual buyer is rarely qualified [by authority and/or expertise] to act as sole negotiator in such situations.' In some cultures, such as Japan, team negotiation is the norm, even if the team does not contribute overtly to the discussion.

There are certain acknowledged advantages to using teams in a range of business and work situations.

- Teams improve performance and decisions.
- Teams facilitate coordination.
- Teams facilitate communication.
- Teams motivate individuals.

Reasons for using teams in negotiations:

- They allow the wider contribution of technical knowledge and interpersonal skills.
- They encourage discussion and information sharing.
- The shared responsibility for outcomes places negotiators under less pressure.
- Team members can back each other up and cover each other's mistakes, if necessary.
- Team members can take different roles in negotiation, to support influencing tactics.

Disadvantages of teams:

- Group decision-making takes longer.
- Group working requires attention to group dynamics and group maintenance processes.
- Team decisions have also been shown to be riskier than individual decisions.
- A variety of viewpoints and specialisms may create a poorly integrated bargaining position.
- Intra-team competition, emulation and status-seeking may add adversarialism to a negotiation.

Virtual meeting options

As an interpersonal process, it is common for negotiations to be conducted face-to-face, enabling the use of non-verbal cues (body language, tone of voice and impressions management, for example) in communication and influencing. However, time and space for negotiation are costly resources, and the value of a negotiation or negotiated outcome will not always justify getting the representatives of both parties together for a face-to-face meeting.

International negotiations are increasingly common, with the globalisation of supply markets, and use of telephone, email, tele-conferencing and web-conferencing negotiation may be the best value option.

Such an option will obviously have to be resourced by the availability (through ownership or rental) of the required equipment and systems.

Although high-value, complex negotiations are likely to be conducted face-to-face, there is a place for the telephone in routine supply negotiations (eg re-buy price adjustments or routine purchase negotiations), especially in the preliminary fact-finding and pre-conditioning stages of the process. Steele emphasises that the phone can be a useful means of conditioning expectations: a supplier proposing a price rise, for example, may make a preliminary telephone call, so that the buyer may be more prepared to accept the proposal when the face-to-face meeting takes place.

A number of factors distinguish telephone negotiation from face-to-face contact.

- Steele *et al* estimate that 75% of information in a negotiation is obtained using non-verbal visual cues: without the benefit of seeing the other party, it is likely that there will be some loss of information.
- Face-to-face negotiation encourages focused attention on the other party. The telephone

may leave the user vulnerable to environmental distractions.

- Telephone negotiation does not enable the shared use of argument-supporting data such as spreadsheets, charts or sample products.
- Steele also cites research suggesting that on the telephone, the stronger case or argument tends to prevail to a greater extent than in face-to-face meetings.
- There tends to be a power advantage to the party that makes the call, who knows the timing and purpose of the call in advance.
- Telephone calls create psychological pressure to conclude a deal before hanging up.
- Problems with technical and/or environmental or background noise may interfere with effective negotiation, if it is difficult for both parties to hear each other clearly.

Virtual face-to-face communication allows organisations to harness the advantages of meetings and discussions *without* having to incur costs of travel, meeting space and so on – and without taking remote or dispersed location (and associated 'home and away' effects) into account.

Web-conferencing and virtual meetings management systems allow negotiators to:

- Conduct 'virtual' face-to-face discussion on teleconference lines, with access to non-verbal cues
- Access real-time product, price, stock and delivery information
- Share pre-prepared multi-media visual aids
- Use electronic 'white boards' for shared brainstorming, visual aids, annotation of data, calculations, note-taking and so on
- Separate desktop displays, so that they can choose which data on their computer display is shared with the other negotiating party, and which is for their own viewing and note-taking only.

Email is now often the preferred medium for communication that would otherwise be carried out face-to-face or on the telephone – and it may be tempting to use it for negotiation (particularly in informal contexts). However, research suggests that email negotiations tend to end in impasse more often than face-to-face or telephone negotiation.

OWN NOTES

OWN NOTES

CHAPTER 11

Stages of Negotiation

Stages of negotiation

In the academic literature, the process of negotiation is often broken down into distinct stages or steps, in a time-phased sequence – and there are many different ways in which this can be done. A representative sample is shown in the table below.

Models of negotiation

KENNEDY	GREENHALGH	BAILY ET AL
Prepare: what do we want?	Preparation	Pre-negotiation phase
Debate: what do they want?	Relationship building	Negotiation or interaction phase
Propose: what wants might we trade?	Information gathering	Post-negotiation follow-up
	Information using	
Bargain: what wants will we trade?	Bidding	
	Closing the deal	
	Implementing the agreement	

A simple overview model suggests three main phases in the negotiation process: pre-negotiation preparation; negotiation/interaction; post-negotiation follow-up.

The use of 'adjournments', or agreements to carry on the negotiation in a separate subsequent meeting, may be an important tactic in allowing one's party to re-group, gather more information and plan new positions and approaches.

Lewicki *et al* also distinguish the stages in an integrative negotiation meeting from those in a distributive negotiation meeting.

- Integrative: identify and define the problem; understand the problem; generate alternative solutions; evaluate and select alternatives; agreement.
- Distributive: selecting an opening offer; selecting an opening stance; gaining and yielding concessions; final offer; agreement.

Planning and preparation

Preparation and planning is central to modern thinking on negotiation, because of the need to:

- Gather adequate information
- Take stakeholder needs and fears into account

11

- Prepare a coherent approach by the negotiating team
- Establish an informed and agreed response to possible contingencies
- Ensure that the team is in agreement as to the minimum terms that will be accepted.

Several stages can be identified in the process of planning a negotiation.

- Defining the **issues**
- Assembling issues and defining the **bargaining mix**
- Defining the **BATNA**
- Defining **interests**
- Defining **limits**
- Defining **objectives and opening bids**
- Defining one's **constituents**
- **Researching and understanding** the other party
- Analysing the **relative bargaining strengths** of the negotiating parties
- Selecting a **strategy**
- **Planning the presentation and defence** of opening positions
- **Defining protocol**
- **Resourcing the meeting**

It is common in cases of very important negotiations to perform a trial run or rehearsal (sometimes called a 'murder court').

Effective behaviours in the preparation phase – negotiators should bear in mind:

- Opportunities for conditioning
- The importance of confidentiality
- Effective team building.

Opening

In the introductory stage it is important to establish the right atmosphere to 'condition' the other party's future responses. Partly this is a matter of physical surroundings. Partly it involves setting the right tone in what is said.

The building of **rapport** is one of the most important tasks of integrative or collaborative negotiation, and a key interpersonal skill for negotiation. Rapport is the sense of relationship or connection we have when we relate to another person. Rapport:

- Helps to establish trust and belief in common ground between you and the other person
- Creates a reason for people to agree with you, or do what you want them to do
- Overcomes some of the barriers created by power imbalances and differences or conflicts of interest.

Frequently there will be an agenda agreed in advance. This prior agreement is important, because negotiators may refuse to discuss issues that confront them for the first time when actually in the meeting room.

Another point to establish early on is who will be recording what is discussed and agreed.

There may be an advantage in volunteering for this role.

A vital component in successful debate or bargaining (especially in positional or distributive negotiation) is the clear and effective statement of each party's opening position. The negotiating team must be adequately prepared to explain its perspective.

In an integrative negotiation, the opening focus will be on collaboratively identifying and defining the problem (or 'presenting issue'). Six elements involved:

- Define the problem in a way that is mutually acceptable to both sides.
- State the problem with an eye toward practicality and comprehensiveness.
- State the problem as a goal and identify the obstacles to attaining this goal.
- Depersonalise the problem.
- Separate the problem definition from the search for solutions.
- Seek to understand the problem, by reference to the underlying interests and needs of each party.

Effective behaviours in the opening phase:

- Rapport building
- Assertive communication
- Using questions to elicit information and clarification from the other party
- Listening actively and effectively
- Facilitating behaviours
- Utilising verbal and non-verbal 'signals' to condition the other party
- Creating an atmosphere conducive to agreement

Testing and proposing

Key tasks in the early phase of negotiation.

- The testing and validation (confirmation) of assumptions made earlier
- Testing the other party's position
- Clarifying the stated issues, and the importance or value given to them by the other party
- Trying to ascertain whether there are any 'surprises' ahead

Baily *et al* observe that: 'You cannot negotiate arguments. No matter how often you argue and disagree with the other side it does not help move forward the negotiation. We would advocate that you make proposals to overcome arguments. In other words, suggest a solution that could overcome the problem.'

Proposals and suggestions, offers and possible solutions to the identified issues, will be put forward for evaluation and discussion at the pre-bargaining stage.

- In a distributive negotiation, proposing may be largely absorbed into bargaining, in the form of offers and counter-offers.
- In an integrative negotiation, it will take the form of a more complex process of generating and evaluating alternative solutions.

11

The **evaluation** of options, according to Lewicki *et al*, involves the following tasks.

- Narrow the range of solution options.
- Evaluate solutions on the basis of quality and acceptability.
- Agree to the criteria for selecting an option in advance of evaluating the options.
- Be willing to provide justification for personal preferences.
- Be alert to the influence of intangible factors.
- Use subgroups to evaluate complex options.
- Take time out to cool off.
- Keep decisions tentative and conditional until the final proposal is complete.
- Minimise formality and record keeping until final agreements are reached.

Three methods of persuasion:

- Appeals to **emotion**
- Appeals to **logic**
- **Threat**

Bargaining

Bargaining is 'the point when we convey the specific terms on which we would settle. For example: "If you reduce your price by 3%, we will increase our order by 10%".

Bargaining is less of a feature of integrative negotiation than of distributive negotiation. In integrative negotiation, having evaluated and selected a range of acceptable options, agreement will often be achieved by bundling together different issues so that all sides will have some issues on which they feel they have reached a good deal.

In the distributive model, purposeful persuasion and constructive compromise are *mainly* achieved through bargaining: the exchange of benefits, currencies and concessions (compromises on one's original position).

To begin with, preparation is vital. The negotiators must have worked out before entering the negotiation how much leeway they are prepared to give on each of the issues to be debated; what 'currencies' and concessions can be cheaply offered to the other party; and what 'currencies' and concessions made by the other party will be acceptable or valuable in return.

An integrative negotiating approach uses concessions to **build trust**. Unilateral or unconditional concessions send the message that ongoing collaboration is a priority, and there is an underlying belief in the potential for mutual satisfaction and gains over time.

A distributive, adversarial or transactional negotiating approach uses concessions as a **trading currency**. Such an approach leads to tactics such as:

- Avoiding being the first party to make a concession (a sign of weakness)
- Making concessions strictly contingent on gaining a concession of equal or greater value
- Making concessions of least possible cost to you

- Giving the impression that every concession you make is a major concession
- Making as few concessions as possible
- Getting the other party to make minor concessions in the early stages

Agreement and closure

Once all the variables have been discussed there comes a point when we may suspect that further progress is impossible. In other words, we conclude that the supplier has nothing more to offer. If we really think there is nothing more to be gained in the negotiation it is time to make a decision.

If our objectives have not been met at this stage, the decision may be simply to walk away. On the other hand, if the overall deal meets our objectives, then it makes sense to shake hands and conclude the agreement.

Once a 'best and final offer' has been made and accepted, the parties have an agreement. The terms still need to be implemented. In some cases, it may be necessary to obtain **ratification**, adoption or endorsement of what has been agreed by an appropriate authority.

The importance of the closure stage can therefore be summarised as follows.

- It ensures that the final summary is as agreed in the negotiation meeting(s).
- It provides a foundation for the ongoing buyer-supplier relationship.
- It provides a tool for gaining stakeholder 'buy in' to the agreement.
- It provides an agenda for action and allocation of responsibilities and accountabilities.
- The minutes or summary acts as a written record and confirmation of the agreement.
- Formally and mutually agreed points can be incorporated into the development of contracts without further discussion.

Once a written agreement is in place, a range of measures may be necessary to ensure that it is **implemented**. It is important to monitor **ongoing performance** of the contract or agreement. Finally, it is beneficial to evaluate the negotiation once it is complete; this provides learning that can help in future negotiations.

11

OWN NOTES

CHAPTER 12

Influencing and Persuasion

Influencing and persuasion

Influencing is the process of applying some form of power or pressure in order to change other people's attitudes or behaviours. **Power** can also be applied to direct people's behaviour in various ways. **Negotiation,** as we have seen, is a process through which two parties come together intentionally to confer with a view to concluding a jointly acceptable agreement.

Influencing is thus different from negotiation in several key respects.

- Influencing is not a single event or series of events: it is a continual process.
- Influencing need not be an intentional (or even conscious) process.
- Influencing need not involve conferring.
- Influencing need not end with an explicit joint agreement.
- Influencing need not involve compromise or movement by both parties.

People's responses to influence attempts take three basic forms.

- **Resistance** means that the other parties position themselves against your request, demand or position, and actively attempt to avoid having to comply.
- **Compliance** means that the other parties are willing to do what is requested or demanded of them, but no more: they make the minimal effort necessary to satisfy the terms of the legal and psychological contract they have agreed to.
- **Commitment** means that the other parties are brought to agree internally with your request, decision or viewpoint: it becomes aligned with their own goals, beliefs and interests, so that they are able to buy into it in a committed way.

Some methods of influencing are more directive (power-based) than others. There are two broad approaches to influencing.

Push influencing and pull influencing

A PUSH APPROACH	A PULL APPROACH
• Exerting power or authority	• Persuasion or interpersonal influence
• Influencees are fully aware of the process, which is overt	• If performed effectively, influencees may not be consciously aware of the process
• Aimed at securing compliance, often against the resistance of influencees	• Can secure commitment, if influencees accept the influencer's proposal or viewpoint as fitting their own goals and interests

12

Methods of persuasion

Persuasion is: 'a means of exerting influence over people by means *other than using authority or power.*' It is the basis of a pull approach to influencing: pulling or leading people to change by bringing their beliefs and goals into alignment with those of the influencer.

Logical argument is essentially a *facilitative* approach, whereby each step of the argument is clearly explained and linked: another key attribute of a 'pull' approach.

Facilitative communication skills include:

- The use of questions and answers, to support information exchange
- Presenting complex arguments in manageable segments
- Summarising each section of a discussion or argument, to reinforce understanding
- Asking for feedback, to check understanding
- Sensitivity and flexibility to respond to verbal and non-verbal signals.

A persuasive negotiation strategy is one which, essentially, seeks to appeal to the needs, goals and interests of the other party.

Techniques of persuasion

TECHNIQUE	EXPLANATION
Threat	Veiled or explicit statements of negative consequences, risks, penalties or sanctions arising from failure to move or comply: suitable only in distributive negotiations, as explicitly adversarial in style.
Emotion	Appeal to supplier goodwill (ingratiation) or emotions about the issue or result eg appeal to fear (of failure, loss or reputational damage) or pride (emphasising status or reputational gains)
Logic	A central tool in most negotiations, based on logical persuasion: carefully marshalling arguments, facts, figures and endorsements in support of a case. If suppliers can be made to agree with each step of a logical argument, it is very difficult for them to say 'no' to the final step of closure (without the psychological discomfort of appearing illogical).
Compromise	Finding the middle ground between buyer and supplier, by moving towards each other's positions: 'meeting each other half way', 'splitting the difference', or making mutual concessions. Often an easy option to push through to closure (and a lose-lose outcome): should only be adopted once the buyer has given up on getting the whole of what it wants.
Bargaining	Extracting value from a deal by the exchange of various items that each party values (currencies).

Influencing tactics

Yukl identified three basic types of influence.

- Impression (or image) management is designed to create or enhance one's credibility and congeniality in the eyes of other people.
- Political influence is designed to gain and apply various forms of power, in order to

influence decisions in favour of one's own (or group) interests.
- Proactive (or ecological) influence is designed to set up conditions in which one is more likely to get the help, support or resources one needs.

Yukl and Falbe identified nine basic influencing tactics: rational persuasion; inspirational appeal; consultation; ingratiation; exchange; personal appeal; coalition; legitimating; and pressure.

Tactics for distributive negotiation:

- Assessing the other party's target outcome, resistance point and costs of terminating the negotiation.
- Managing the other party's impressions and assumptions about one's *own* target outcomes, resistance point and costs of withdrawal.
- Changing or re-framing the supplier's perceptions
- Manipulating the costs of delaying agreement or terminating a negotiation.

Tactics for integrative negotiation:

- Expanding the pie
- Log-rolling
- Non-specific compensation
- Cutting the costs of compliance
- Bridging

Pushing for closure in distributive negotiations:

- Provide alternatives
- Assume the close
- Split the difference
- Exploding offer
- Sweeteners

Behavioural technologies

Perhaps the best known of the behavioural technologies is neuro-linguistic programming (NLP), which seeks to help people to:

- Understand how sensory perception and language influence behaviour
- Utilise techniques based on the ability of thoughts, language and sensory cues to change or reinforce behaviour
- Act more intentionally to produce the results they want in their own behaviours and in their interactions with other people.

Mainstream technologies established by the developers of NLP:

- Preferred information-processing channels
- Mirroring
- Pacing and leading
- Anchoring
- Mental rehearsal

12

- Framing and re-framing
- Positioning
- Intentional use of language to shift thought and behaviour patterns

If you are on the *receiving* end of such technologies, one approach to avoiding being manipulated by them is known as the 'ABC' process.

- **A**cknowledge it for what it is
- **B**reak down the content (to analyse how you are being manipulated)
- **C**hallenge it: 'That would seem to imply that there are only two options, but in fact, there's another possibility' – and so on.

Ethical influencing

Four sources of moral standards which might guide a negotiator's thinking about the desired outcomes of negotiation, and how to go about influencing others to achieve them.

- End-results ethics
- Rule ethics
- Social contract ethics
- Personal ethics

OWN NOTES

OWN NOTES

CHAPTER 13

Communication Skills for Negotiation

Behaviours of skilled negotiators

In regard to **pre-negotiation planning**, successful negotiators:

* Consider a wider range of outcomes or options for action
* Give more attention to anticipated areas of common ground and possible agreement
* Think more about the long-term implications of issues
* Set objectives within a range of upper and lower limits
* Plan around issues, without attempting to link them in a sequence

In regard to **face-to-face negotiatory meetings,** successful negotiators:

* Use behaviour labelling
* Ask more questions
* Summarise and test understanding
* Comment on feelings: establishing transparency to inspire trust
* Use fewer 'irritators'
* Use fewer immediate counter-proposals
* Avoid 'defend-attack spirals'
* Avoid diluting their argument by piling up multiple justifications

In regard to **post-negotiation follow-up**, skilled negotiators set aside time to reflect on their performance and what they have learned from it.

Attempts to describe personality focus on two broad concepts.

* Personality **traits**
* Personality **types**

Lewicki *et al* summarise six different ways in which researchers have purported to find stable differences between men and women negotiators.

* Relational view of others
* Embedded view of agency
* Beliefs about ability and worth
* Control through empowerment
* Problem solving through dialogue
* Perceptions and stereotypes

13

Interpersonal and communication skills

Supply chain relationships require 'people skills'.

- **Interpersonal skills** are used in interactions between two or more people.
- **Intrapersonal skills** involve processes within an individual.

Negotiators require a broad repertoire of communication skills.

- Probing (using questions effectively to elicit information)
- Active listening
- Expressing empathy
- Communicating assertively
- Building and maintaining rapport
- Focusing on interpersonal processes
- Using and interpreting non-verbal cues (body language and tone of voice)

The core skill-set of emotional intelligence (EQ) includes being aware of, or sensitive to, the needs and emotions of other people – and being able to respond flexibly to those needs and emotions in such a way as to build relationships and get the best out of people.

What is communicated during negotiation?

- Offers and counter-offers
- Information about alternatives
- Information about outcomes
- Social accounts
- Communications about process

Key **rapport-building techniques**:

- Subtly matching or 'mirroring' the other person's posture, body language etc
- Picking up on the other person's use of technical words, colloquialisms and metaphors
- Picking up on the other person's dominant way of experiencing and expressing things
- Listening attentively and actively to what the other person is saying
- Finding topics of common interest, and identifying areas of agreement
- Remembering and using people's names

Daniel Goleman has popularised the argument that leadership success does not only depend on technical ability and mental dexterity (IQ), but on emotional awareness and maturity. Higgs and Reynolds have adapted this model for a procurement setting as follows.

- **Self-awareness:** the awareness of your own feelings and the ability to recognise and manage these
- **Emotional resilience:** being able to perform well and consistently in a range of situations and when under pressure
- **Motivation:** the drive and energy which you have to achieve results, to balance short-term and long-term goals, and to pursue your goals in the face of challenge and rejection
- **Interpersonal sensitivity**: the ability to be aware of the needs and feelings of others
- **Influence:** the ability to persuade others to change their viewpoint

- **Intuitiveness:** the ability to use insight and interaction
- **Conscientiousness and integrity:** the ability to display commitment to a course of action in the face of challenge, to act consistently

Effective listening

Listening is a key activity in any negotiation. The activity of listening includes two basic processes: hearing and interpreting.

Barriers to effective listening include selective listening and adaptive listening.

Three basic modes of listening: passive, acknowledging and active.

- **Passive listening** is a style of listening which implies hearing, but without any attempt to engage the other person.
- **Acknowledging** is a style of listening which indicates basic attentiveness by giving feedback signals to show the other person that you are listening.
- **Active listening** is a listening style which fully uses the feedback potential of verbal communication.

Active listening is helpful in:

- Facilitating understanding, by encouraging the other person to give information
- Encouraging more open, honest and spontaneous communication
- Facilitating understanding
- Facilitating subsequent recall of the message
- Building initial rapport and subsequent collaborative relationships.

Active listening behaviours include:

- Building rapport
- Signalling attentiveness and interest
- Signalling empathy
- Engaging actively in the process
- Being alert to perceptual bias
- Giving encouraging and clarifying feedback
- Paying attention to non-verbal cues and processes

Characteristics of effective listeners:

- Non-verbal behaviour
- Focus of attention
- Acceptance
- Empathy
- Probing
- Paraphrasing
- Summarising

13

Using questions

Lewicki *et al* highlight the fact that questions may be used:

- To elicit information
- To uncover deception, manipulation, inconsistency, evasion and other flaws
- To refocus an integrative negotiation and generate win-win options
- To build rapport and trust, by encouraging the exchange of information.

Types of question:

- Open questions
- Closed questions
- Probing questions
- Multiple questions
- Leading questions
- Reflective questions
- Hypothetical questions

Non-verbal communication

Non-verbal communication is – simply – communication without words. Research suggests that we convey more than half of the meaning of any given spoken message via non-verbal signals, other than the words themselves.

There is a wide variety of non-verbal 'cues'.

- **Kinesic behaviour** (or 'body language'): movements such as gestures, facial expressions, eye contact and body posture
- **Proxemics:** how near you stand or sit to others, whether you lean toward or away, what space or barriers you place between you
- **Paralanguage:** tone of voice, speed, emphasis and other vocal qualities
- **Object language:** personal grooming, dress, furniture and symbols.

It is important to be aware that no single non-verbal cue is sufficient to make an accurate diagnosis of someone's meaning or mental state. This is particularly important in cross-cultural communication, because the use and interpretation of body language may differ significantly from one culture to another.

In addition to the spoken word, non-verbal communication techniques are also powerful mechanisms for assisting the *influencing* process.

- **Eye contact**: failure to make consistent eye contact suggests dishonesty; but it would be inappropriate to make too much eye contact: this comes across as staring, and may be perceived as threatening.
- **Adjusting body position**: to show attention, it is important to adopt an appropriate body position; slouching suggests lack of attention or interest; turning away may suggest rudeness.

- **Non-verbal encouragement or discouragement**: slight nodding of the head, murmurs of approval or interest, hand gestures encouraging the speaker to continue can all convey agreement or at least engagement with the other party.

The influence of culture

Cross-cultural or international negotiations will be complicated by factors such as:

- Differences in negotiating styles
- Differences in conflict-handling styles
- Differences in language
- Differences in non-verbal cues

Hofstede identified five dimensions along which various cultures differed from each other.

- **Power distance**: the extent to which the unequal distribution of power is accepted by members of a society.
- **Uncertainty avoidance:** how much members of a society are threatened by uncertain and ambiguous situations.
- **Individualism-collectivism**: the tendency to take care of oneself and one's family versus the tendency to work together for the collective good.
- **Masculinity-femininity**: the extent to which highly assertive masculine values predominate, as opposed to sensitivity and concern for others' welfare.
- **Long-term orientation**: the extent to which thrift and perseverance are valued (long-term orientation) over respect for tradition, fulfilling solid obligations and protecting one's 'face' (short-term orientation).

Many aspects of negotiation are likely to be affected by the position of a particular culture within these dimensions.

- The selection of negotiators
- The agenda for the negotiation
- The timetable for negotiation
- The tactics and styles of negotiation

Edward Hall suggested that another dimension of cultural difference is the extent to which the content and understanding of communication is influenced by its context: non-verbal aspects, underlying implications, interpersonal factors and so on.

- **Low-context** cultures (eg Germanic, Scandinavian, North American) tend to take the content of communication at face value: words say what they mean. They prefer clear, written, explicit communication.
- **High-context** cultures (eg Japanese, Asian, African, Latin American, Middle-Eastern, Southern European) interpret and exchange more complex messages. They prefer face-to-face and oral communication, and are good at developing networks and using non-verbal cues and unspoken implications.

13

Acuff highlights a number of ways in which negotiations differ from one culture to another.

- The **pace of negotiation** is more rapid in North America than in most other cultures.
- **Negotiation strategies** differ too. In some countries (Acuff suggests Russia, Egypt and China) extensive haggling is the norm. In other countries, such as Australia and Sweden, the opening bid and the final settlement will tend to be very close.
- The emphasis on **personal relationships** is more pronounced in some cultures than others.
- The use of **emotion** is regarded as normal in some cultures (eg Latin America), but tends to arouse distrust in other cultures (eg in Switzerland or Germany).
- There are important differences in methods of **decision making**.
- Finally, there are differences in **contractual and administrative factors**.

Acuff highlights a number of additional problems faced by negotiators in international settings: that is, negotiations which take place outside their own country of origin and operation.

- **Culture shock**
- **Negotiating with one's own boss** can be difficult if he does not appreciate that things may develop differently from a home negotiation.
- **Resolving ethical issues** may be difficult in countries where hospitality and gifts are an accepted part of the culture
- The decision of whether to meet **home or away** is more critical.

OWN NOTES

OWN NOTES

CHAPTER 14

Developing Negotiation Performance

Reflecting on negotiation performance

Evaluating a negotiation need not wait until the end of the process.

- **Formative** (process-focused) evaluation may be carried out before negotiation or during negotiation.
- **Summative** (process- and outcome-focused) evaluation may be carried out *after* negotiation, in order to extract learning for future negotiations.

Maylor points out that learning can be captured from projects (and negotiations) both **by doing** (drawing on the formative and summative evaluation of past experience) and **before doing** (by applying prior preparation and external knowledge, such as this course).

The outcome of the evaluation should be a written record including:

- A comparison of actual outcomes achieved with the objectives originally set
- A review of the agreement achieved
- An evaluation of the performance of negotiators
- A checklist of points learned for use in future negotiations.

Tools for structured reflection

David Kolb's **experiential learning cycle** shows how everyday work experiences can be used for learning, personal development and performance improvement, through the process of 'learning by doing'.

Other useful tools for reflecting on negotiation performance:

- The use of a personal development journal
- The use of critical incident analysis
- Formal post-negotiation review and evaluation
- The seeking of feedback (formal or informal) on your own performance in a negotiation
- The monitoring of post-negotiation behaviour

The outcomes of negotiation to be evaluated, in order to appraise its success, include:

- The content or task-based outcomes of the negotiation
- The satisfaction, commitment and compliance of both parties

14

- The state of the relationship between the two parties at the end of the negotiation.

Opportunities for improvement and development

Some learning or training requirements for negotiation may emerge relatively informally in the course of work.

- Changes in legislation, technology or work methods create a knowledge or skill gap.
- Critical incidents may be observed or reported and then analysed.
- Developmental discussions may be used to focus on the individual's goals for improvement and identify interventions needed to attain them.
- Self-assessment and personal development activities may lead individuals to identify areas in which they are not satisfied with their performance.

Learning or training needs analysis involves:

- Measuring what employees need to be *able* to do
- Measuring what employees actually *can* do
- Identifying any 'gap' between the two.

Methods and media for learning and development of negotiation performance:

- On-the-job (such as instruction, coaching and experiential learning through practice in negotiation, reflection and feedback)
- Off-the-job (such as taught classes and workshops, the use of case studies and role plays, and e-learning)
- Formal (such as courses, planned coaching, negotiation and influencing skills training and so on)
- Informal (such as picking up information from reading, watching how others negotiate, or getting informal advice and feedback from co-workers or managers).

Post-negotiation relationship management

Negotiation, contracting and contract award are *not* the end of the story. Buyers must also be concerned with contract management and supplier relationship management.

The key processes and activities involved in contract management:

- Contract development: the formulation of contracts
- Contract administration: implementing buyer-side and supplier-side procedures to ensure that contract obligations are fulfilled
- Managing contract performance
- Contract review
- Relationship management
- Contract renewal or termination

If contracts are not well managed the following adverse outcomes may occur.

- The supplier may be obliged to take control of contract performance and problem-solving

- Decisions may not be taken at the right time (or at all).
- Buyer and supplier may fail to understand their obligations and responsibilities.
- There may be misunderstandings and disagreements.
- Progress may be slow, or there may be an inability to move forward.
- The intended benefits and value from the contract may not be realised.
- Opportunities to improve value for money and performance may be missed.

Value-adding benefits of positive contract management:

- Improved risk management in developing and managing contracts
- Improved compliance and commitment by the supplier
- Incentives and momentum for ongoing relationship development and performance improvement
- Better value for money (arising from efficient contract administration and performance)

Value-adding benefits to the positive and proactive management of supplier relationships:

- The company incurs fewer costs of identifying, appraising and training new vendors.
- Quality and other problems can be ironed out progressively.
- Goodwill developed with positive relationships may earn preferential treatment or flexibility from suppliers in the event of emergencies.
- Suppliers may be more motivated to give their best performance.
- Motivated suppliers may be willing to co-invest.
- There is less risk of supplier failure or poor performance.

After the sourcing, selecting and contracting of suppliers, therefore, it remains the buyer's responsibility:

- To maintain regular contact with the supplier
- To monitor the supplier's performance against the agreed terms and standards
- To motivate the supplier
- To work with the supplier to solve any performance problems
- To work with the supplier to resolve any relationship problems or disputes

One way of getting more out of supplier relationships is to improve supplier commitment, co-operation and loyalty. This can be done in a number of ways.

- Supplier motivation and performance management
- Ensuring that there are meaningful incentives for performance and relationship improvement
- Maintaining positive, relationship-building contacts and communications
- Securing the commitment and sponsorship of senior managers in both organisations
- Cultivating personal contacts and networks, building trust and goodwill on each side
- Ethical, constructive, collaborative and, where possible, 'win-win' negotiation to resolve relationship and performance problems
- Being an attractive customer (or avoiding being an *un*attractive customer), by maintaining a sufficient volume of business to justify suppliers' investment in the relationship *and* by maintaining ethical, co-operative, efficient, professional and congenial dealings with suppliers

- Engaging suppliers in co-investment and co-development: collaborative product development, planning and training; systems integration; gain sharing; and so on
- Ensuring that the principles of reciprocity, mutual benefit or 'win-win' are observed as far as possible